EMERITUS

BRIAN COX (as C.B. Cox) co-edited the controversial *Black Papers on Education* (1969–77) and chaired the National Curriculum English Working Group (1988–9). His book on National Curriculum English, *Cox on Cox* (1991), became a best-seller. In 1993 he retired as John Edward Taylor Professor of English Literature at Manchester University, after serving as Dean of the Faculty of Arts (1984–6) and Pro-Vice Chancellor (1987–91). He has published books of literary criticism and an autobiography, and has edited anthologies and collections of essays. He was a founder editor of *Critical Quarterly*. After retirement he chaired the Arvon Foundation for three years and the North West Arts Board for six, including two years as a member of the Arts Council. In retirement he edited a two-volume collection of essays, *African Writers*, for Scribners, and wrote a second book on the National Curriculum (*The Battle for the English Curriculum*, 1995). He remains poetry editor of *Critical Quarterly*.

BRIAN COX

Emeritus

CARCANET

First published in 2001 by
Carcanet Press Limited
4th Floor, Conavon Court
12-16 Blackfriars Street
Manchester M3 5BQ

A CIP catalogue record for this book
is available from the British Library
ISBN 1 85754 544 3

The publisher acknowledges financial assistance
from the Arts Council of England

Set in 12pt Bembo by Bryan Williamson, Frome
Printed and bound in England by SRP Ltd, Exeter

Contents

Acknowledgements

Acknowledgements are due to editors of the following journals: *Critical Quarterly* for 'A Bullet at the Wedding', 'Saul Bellow', 'Rebirth in Cyprus', 'Lanzarote' and 'The Grand Hotel, Taiwan'; *The Hudson Review* for 'Musée d'Orsay'; *The Kenyon Review* for 'Fishes and Ladders'; *London Magazine* for 'Cape of Good Hope'; *PN Review* for 'Emeritus', 'Humberside Funeral' and 'Welbeck Abbey, 1948'; *Poetry Review* for 'Amis and Larkin'; *The Sewanee Review* for 'Liverpool', 'Lyme Lady' and 'Quinta del Sordo'. 'Kinder Trespass' was published in *Poetry in the Parks: A Celebration of the National Parks of England and Wales in Poems and Photographs* (2000), edited by Wendy Bardsley.

Emeritus

And so I retired,
apprenticed to silence,
only one deadline to meet,
no worries at 6 a.m.,
ambition obsolete;
cv permanently filed,
sleep easy as a child.

In sunlit woods near Albi
a fisherman in green waders,
older than me,
casts his line for trout.
I find the June camps empty;
banished from academe
I dine beside a dappled stream.

He doesn't speak or even smile;
hours of silence pass,
prodigiously futile;
ripples reveal abundant fish
he fails to catch, and then
while I read Yeats, taking stock,
his line snags on a sunken rock.

He treads swift-running waters
gingerly: fears a slip.
Enlivened by his plight
when he decides to quit
I feel a sense of fellowship;
in quiet pastoral retreat
we both admit one more defeat.

Next day beside the water's edge
I chew high-fibre bran.
Above the far bank's hedge
jogs a two-pronged pole
borne by my fisherman;
still granting me no sign
he soon retrieves his line.

Humberside Funeral

After the funeral I mix
gossip and politics

with friends I used to know
thirty, forty years ago.

Old faces in a double sense
force me to serial pretence,

as I shake hands with those
whose youthful postures froze

in scenes from post-war Hull.
I burrow deep to half recall

a girl I once thought sweet,
now hobbling on arthritic feet.

She looks straight in my eyes,
and suddenly the distance dies;

her nature floods the years between,
as if lost time had never been.

Although I can't rake up her name,
we're all the same: no one has changed.

Heron

I see myself seeing
this true landscape painting:

surprising grey heron,
at home in my garden,

its black crest, yellow bill,
poised and sentinel-still.

I watch myself being
watched inside the painting:

the heron is no symbol,
no guardian angel,

just a bird whose vision
helps me to envision

a godlike state seeing
myself as a painting.

My heron, legs trailing,
flies off from my watching,

bird from never-never,
fragile but for ever.

Saul Bellow

You won't remember me;
we dined together once
at BR's Grand Hotel.
My wife was pregnant;
when you left you wished her well.

And now the bulge you once
addressed with so much charm
is thirty-eight, a mother too;
maybe great men's words
make miracles come true.

That week you dreamt Herzog:
for him pain burnt slow like green wood.
He wrote letters he never sent
to Eisenhower, to shrinks,
and once or twice to God.

At Ludeyville, his mansion
left to rot after divorce,
he heard fierce music of birds,
felt the pull of common life,
an idiot joy, too great for words.

He didn't end his argument
with God, or find a brief for pain,
yet knew a love impulse,
natural to man, as grass
produces green or wheat its grain.

A Bullet at the Wedding

Ten years ago
in Cheadle Hulme
bright banquet rooms –
ghosts wait to be touched.

Fathers of bride and groom
we tip back German hock;
perched side by side
we share no language.

Whispers from long ago
ride each wedding toast;
for me it's Grimsby raids,
ack–ack, whistling bombs

dropped by your comrades.
For you it's that Russian slug
still lodged in your head;
three feet away its presence,

swathed in flesh and blood,
haunts our every glance.
The guests know your story;
behind their eyes pictures form –

the banquet room aswarm
with memories of war.
But now in time of peace
although no one may shake

your stricken right arm
(your meat cut by your niece)
our children's fingers intertwine
to slice the wedding cake.

All this ten years ago:
beneath my apple trees I hear
our grandson's words combine
pure English for my family,

fluent German for his friends,
unaware he's changed the text.
Now we witness miracles:
Humber flows into the Rhine.

Cape of Good Hope

Made for Union, the Cape combines
all colours and all scents.
I drink fruity wines
grown on fragrant slopes
where no apartheid splits
yellowwood from chestnut trees,
orchids from wild iris flowers:
paradise I think should breed
home for every race and creed.

White guest of old white friends,
I look for paradise regained,
a Cape where segregation ends . . .
Instead they talk of coons;
in white Cape-Dutch mansions
Alsatians are still trained to maul blacks.
Servants banished to the sticks
won't have long to brood and wait
before their turn to dominate.

Violence quickens everywhere.
At mid-day in a crowded square
muggers tug my coat, finger me.
I clutch my wallet, and they run,
afraid I tote a hidden gun.
Then traffic slows and blue lights flash;
in England I'd expect a crash.
Here it's car theft, a common episode:
the driver's body lies beside the road.

Castleton

By Peveril Castle, Cave Dale,
ice-cold streams and slippery rocks,
I step along an upland trail
to pasture land and finger post.

Under a sky of changing greys
I skirt by Dirtlow Rake, sheep folds,
old mines whose lead brought working men
to make for us these bridleways.

Back at the car, I change my boots.
Bare feet cool down in nippy air,
a joy so sharp it changes round
a day that started in despair.

Liverpool Cathedrals

Cathedral confronts cathedral;
battleships sail over city roofs

joined by misnamed Hope Street,
clobbered now by driving sleet.

The parking lot a jail,
my Ford, windows steamed up,

rocks to rhythms of the gale.
Crouched in my seat I think

a cherub from mappa mundi
with puffed cheeks angrily

batters cathedral stone
to turn each throne to dust

so we might build again
one church, one community.

At last the storm abates;
on the horizon a chink of blue.

I wipe inside windows,
meet a dropout's watery eyes

matted hair everywhere,
brown coat like a dishevelled bear

under a green golf umbrella.
He raps the pane, and I donate a coin.

He leaps in the air,
umbrella waved aloft,

hops away across the square,
dancing, unemployed,

between cathedrals and the void.

Kinder Trespass

Descending moorland paths through mist,
I peer ahead to spot the marker stone.
A week-day hike, I'm quite alone,
until two boys on mountain bikes appear,

jumping their wheels over earth clods,
bumping and gliding through the clouds.
Across a green-scum bog a wooden bridge
leads to an ancient shooting lodge,

a white hut eerie in the drifting light.
History lives one pace beyond my sight:
country gentlemen, majors, brigadiers,
their entourage of fearsome gamekeepers.

Sixty years ago at William Clough
they confronted Benny Rothman, cyclist,
who dodged police out for his arrest
by pedalling all the way from Manchester.

From city slums each young male rambler
took bike or train to open moors,
to cock a snook at trespass laws,
and wade at will each slimy peatland trail.

Hayfield police awaited their return,
dragged Benny and five more to Leicester jail,
incarcerated many months
so gentlemen might shoot wild birds.

Mist thickens, histories retreat;
through kissing gates I tramp to Hayfield,
where in a small café I meet
the bikers guzzling giant mugs of tea.

Dervish

Across the Anatolian plain
I'm driven to a village sanctuary:
an ill-lit room, a small fountain.
Uneasy on a low, purple divan,
I wait the advent of the holy man.

At my feet lie Turkish carpets,
arabesques of tendril and vine,
tigers, peacocks, nightingales,
designs whose music transforms
my city life to distant fantasy.

I'm here to see his paintings,
but first he offers Muslim courtesy,
formal greetings and the rites of tea.
He speaks no English, but smiles at me,
dips his long bamboo flute in the pool

to soften the tone, and then plays
arabesques of tendril and vine.
I do not understand his credo,
but as I catch his eye I know
we share messages and melodies

woven from the other side of time.

Rebirth in Cyprus

When Christ released him from the grave,
Lazarus took flight across the seas
to found this church at Larnaka;
here in its dark and fusty nave
an acolyte bids me to wear

a dark-blue smock to hide my knees.
I feel arrayed for sacrifice,
forced for half an hour to bear
his talk of hell and paradise;
worse still, to see in every phrase

the winding sheets of puritans
wrapped round my adolescent days.
Icons of black and gold-leafed saints
glower at me in the half-light.
How can I escape restraints

thrust so deep into my mind
by years of hell-fire declamation?
Among the jumbled saints I find
Lazarus at the exit to his tomb;
disgusted by the charnel smell

a bystander pinches tight his nose.
At once laughter like a bell
carols an end to haloes.
Outside along the beach I join
April crowds who sweat and smell

and laugh and love in Larnaka.
At ease in motley bathing gear
they look on pleasure as their right.
My smock discarded in the porch
I'm born again in Cyprus light.

Athos in Paphos

Past almond blossom, carob tree and vine
we drive from Limassol to Paphos;
we dine outdoors near fishing boats
and share meze: taramosalata,
houmous, kleftiko, mousaka,
words I enjoy more than Greek food,
washed down with tepid Aphrodite wine.

Afterwards, sun and wine dazed,
we hover in tourist stores,
sad doodads and geegaws,
international bric-a-brac.
I find among a stack of saints
a gold and red Last Supper,
a strange, unsettling luminosity.

The haloed Christ glares centre stage;
disciples highlight shock
as if winds from nowhere rock
the festive table's bread and wine.
Betrayal for them, for me a magic sign,
splendour through the craft of monks,
welcome contrast to our modern age.

Outside the traffic growls and bays;
I clutch my purchase, pleased to own
this replica contrived by unknown
celibates who at Mount Athos paint
haloes for each prayerful saint:
silent hours of rumination,
shadowed by beach and ilex trees.

In letters home Edward Lear
told London friends how he drew
and gawped in wonder at each Athos view,
filled his saddle-bags
with sketches of monasteries on crags,
but plied his wit on chanting monks,
their days reduced to parrot prayer.

His badinage recalls for me
Athos monks abhor females;
their manic faith entails
import of tom-cats to kill mice:
cock and mule rule this paradise
whose so-called saints flee their wives,
seeking pure tranquillity.

Their art depends on sacrifice.
I choose the rags and mess of life,
intimacy of man and wife,
votaries of golden Aphrodite,
her Paphos temple of fertility.
That night we join the tourists,
seduced maybe by merchandise;

but like Lear's owl and pussycat,
we play to a common tune,
actors in endless comedy:
hand in hand by the edge of the sand
we stroll by the light of the moon.

Lanzarote

'Action is consolatory.' Joseph Conrad

In Lanzarote at Jameos del Agua
we descend below the sunlit world;
in tourist caves we explore
an ancient green lake where
white blind crabs, a rare species,
teeter about the sandy floor.

I wonder what I'm doing here,
retired, on winter holiday,
wasting time with miniscule crabs.
I don't need pastimes when time is short;
later, as we drive our hired Ford
across heaped-up volcanic slabs,

bare and ugly as northern slag heaps,
I'm depressed. At Timanfaya
we watch an aproned Spanish boy
fry spitting eggs on earth heat.
Water is poured into an iron pipe;
steam shoots into the air. What joy!

Back in sunny Puerto del Carmen
we drift into a cheap bazaar.
Squinting in the shadowy doorway,
I'm cross when two louts jostle me,
then suddenly wake up to feel
my money wallet slide away.

Outside a young man starts to flee.
I still can sprint, so chase behind,
shouting 'Stop thief' to Spanish walls.
As I begin to overtake
he throws my wallet on the ground,
dodges away through market stalls.

I count my cash and credit cards.
When I look up the youth has paused,
bent panting thirty yards ahead.
He smiles at me, a gentle smile,
as if we're linked by some conspiracy,
then slides behind a lean-to shed.

Back in the shop I've not been missed.
My wife buys gifts for grandchildren,
mementoes of this sundrenched isle.
Aged voyeur of crabs and eggs,
I feel renewed, bearing my spoils:
adventures and an eerie smile.

Welbeck Abbey, 1948

The mad fifth Duke
loved his underworld,
hid away his fear
below the fields' veneer.

His Irish workmen,
refugees from famine,
dug under our feet
private street after street,

a sunken ballroom,
criss-cross of tunnels,
so he could walk unseen
beneath the English green.

After our war, Welbeck
housed old soldiers,
young in crafts of peace,
waiting their release.

We studied to build,
at night caroused,
wasting hours before
at last an open door.

Outside a long calm,
silence of the guns;
We thought we'd found
stable English ground.

Instead new wars:
Korea, Ireland, Bosnia;
cities reduced to ruin,
green fields paper thin.

Saturday Late in Manchester

At night through gargoyle streets
crowds dance postmodern beats,

while I walk sharply to my car,
loving and hating this brouhaha.

The masks of youth convey
identities both straight and gay;

men with Cantona shirts embrace
girls who hide a nymphette grace

behind their black space-age gear,
downing pints of Greenall's beer.

Forty cumbersome years too old,
I walk away into the cold,

past All Saints park where piles of rag
disgorge a sodden scallywag

who offers me *Big Issue* tracts.
When I reject his artifacts

he speaks to me, waggles his head:
'You ought to be tucked up in bed.'

Musée d'Orsay

In a converted railway hall
three floors of escalators climb
to Monet, Gauguin and Van Gogh.

Opposite my chin, riding the steps,
a hawk-nosed woman past her prime
— tight, short skirt, multi-coloured blouse,

dresses like a maypole sheath.
As we slowly rise in line she
kisses her bald swain on the lips,

slips her tongue between his teeth.
Forced to goggle from underneath,
we're an old couple in flat-soled shoes,

comely vestments for Paris walks,
wondering if we're meant to watch
these ostentatious bills and coos.

We find the galleries ablaze,
Van Gogh's swirling greens, angry blues,
rich colour burning in our eyes.

I stand near the maypole to see
Gauguin's child bride nude on her bed,
his rage against propriety.

If we all jettisoned restraint
would we unlock an earthly paradise?
His picture lives within its frame and style;

our passion thrives on privacy,
a force so rare it might be shown in paint,
but not by gestures in a public hall.

Wheelchair Dancers

We robot guests obey
conventions duly grey;

we're watching U Cando
like patrons at a zoo;

palsy does not restrain
nor paralysis enchain

as wheel-chairs back and fro
perform capriccio.

While we drool good-will words,
their spit flies up like birds.

Journey to Simla

Half way up the mountain
the rackety coach stops:

quick sips of scalding tea
served in dirty, cracked cups.

An old-fashioned Hindu
bends to kiss my dusty shoe.

A youth shares my disgust,
smiles at my confusion.

In mountain light his eyes
glow new-Indian and free;

through light cloud I see where
Simla hills leap upwards:
white peaks poised in blue air.

Amis and Larkin

Amis told Larkin he
asked every pretty she

to favour him in bed.
'One out of four,' he said,

succumbed to his request.
Larkin was not impressed:

'But what about the three –
the ones who won't agree?'

He couldn't play that game.
'The shame,' he wailed, 'the shame.'

Traffic

Letters posted, I touch
the sign to cross the road.

I'm told to 'Wait', while round
the bend a coffin-load

of flowers leads limousines
towards lights now red.

What else is there to do?
I give the waiting dead

a half-salute, and then
while mourners glare, walk on.

Lyme Lady

The barge beneath the distant hill
appears to me completely still.

It moves, I know, with stately mien,
through diverse shades of blue and green.

Its owners steer their way like lords
slowly and silently towards,

towards, some paradise maybe,
but here and now is all I see,

for on the tow-path where I stand
they greet me from their promised land:

In dappled light our voices blend,
transforming stranger into friend.

Sad Song

The widow chants her grief at evening
in her grange by the drear canal;

(the anglers hear her distant keening,
but find her lonely song banal).

She touches her piano lightly,
(the anglers weigh their catch in scales)

singing of loved ones lost at sea;
(the anglers walk the pub-bound trails).

She shapes herself as prima donna,
takes pleasure from her serenade;

(they know she'll find another lover:
time heals and cannot be delayed).

Fishes and Ladders

Caught in nets of sense, under branches,
my eyes reflect both light and dark;
fish under trees, goggle eyes astare,
create afresh green leaves, grey bark.

Swim where I may, under birch or palm,
my distances for ever fade;
I must become what I behold,
tangled empirically in shade.

If only trees would turn to ladders,
break the surface, mount on high;
but modern Jonahs prefer their whale;
modern fish will never fly.

At death, suddenly, the birds descend,
thrush at my throat, dove as my crown;
pecking at eyes they sing in chorus;
the marvel opens, the sky falls down.

Hysterectomy

(after Coleridge's 'Ancient Mariner')

Beside the ancient kissing gate
a scrawny shepherd's bright blue eye
affixes me to moorland turf;
no fearful Wedding Guest am I,
but too unsure and too polite
to push aside his urgent tale.

One night, he says, he drove home late
so soggy-brained with lambing chores
he fell upon his lonely bed
before he'd shut the barnyard doors:
his bitch in heat was left to find
a midnight suitor at her side.

The birth was hard: four pups dragged out,
three limp and dead, one just alive,
and soon inside the womb the vet
detected foetus number five.
Trying to tell what happened next,
the shepherd could not quite recall

the word I gave him like a charm
to loose once more his simple tale.
After the op the bitch stayed sick,
for months confined to haunt the farm
until this day when slow but true
she crouched beside the shepherd's flock.

I touch his arm, bid him adieu,
then tramp away across the field.
When I look back, he hasn't moved;
he doesn't need my language skill:
no sanctimonious priest
can shrive him of his clinging guilt.

He prayeth well who loveth well
both man and bird and beast.

Signs

I've learnt to love frail signs in snow,
footsteps that tell where wild things go;

at dawn I trace the necklace path
across the garden's pure white cloth

of dainty fox whose midnight bark
troubles the silence of our park.

On walks I note the trail of mole,
the pheasant's splendid straight patrol;

so pigeons, weasels, mice betray
their nightly paths to light of day.

Waiting

One more autumn sunrise,
yet today I can see

old gardens in new guise;
spaces form shapes, empty

only to frozen eyes.
From nothings I create

visions between hollyhocks;
I dare to contemplate

time behind ancient clocks,
and still, though old, await

a glimpse of urban fox,
the postman at the gate.

Van Gogh in Holland

As the sun sets
windmills shine.

He looks
through eye-lashes:
nervous – all that colour.

No more analysis,
no more
sharp structures;

just downiness
of clouds,
delicate lilac sky;

just a heath at twilight:
peat barges
drawn by white horses;

just cottages rising
out of the earth:
moss-covered roofs.

Beyond eye-lashes
colours shape his sight:
the simplest things.

Impressions of Zola

His father's dam fed fountains in Aix;
its shadow fell across the orphan boy
who, with Cézanne, hiked hobbledehoy
the slopes of Sainte Victoire, heard each hour
the parish bells stirring the drowsy air.

To beat the shadow back he trod tiptoe
through talismans, touching a special oak
to ward off evil sprites, making a joke
of magic numbers: always a slave
to omens springing from his father's grave.

His novels circumscribe commotion:
over his father's dam the waters spill
to feed canals; force subject to the will;
beneath tents of summer foliage
din of rapids down Infernet gorge.

So Nana: glowing like a sun-queen she
bestrides the crowds at Longchamps, champagne
held high to celebrate her brief acclaim,
riding the mob roar from a thousand throats:
for Zola wild beasts under frock coats.

At home he cherished paraphernalia.
He craved for medieval bric-à-brac,
each objet d'art an almanac
foretelling fate through alabaster clocks,
dented pewter, Aubusson antiques.

Behind a polished monumental desk,
pernickety about his daily health.
his substance swelled together with his wealth;
Cézanne felt like a suitor forced to wait,
nervous before a minister of state.

So Dreyfus and *J'accuse*: why intervene?
Old beasts had broken down the barriers,
fouled clear streams with the scum of sewers:
for him language could restore an ordered flow,
force truth on this imbroglio.

After threats against his life, a fixed trial,
anti-Dreyfusards made Zola hide
at Summerfield in Addlestone; he lived
deprived of language, his rich furniture,
as if in this time of great discomfiture

the green curtain of English countryside
divided him from all his just demesnes.
He soon refound his love of detailed scenes;
England could never make a second home
but after cycling through the honeycomb

of Surrey's undulating, tree-lined lanes
he described to Jeanne, his youthful mistress,
erotic views of lady cyclists,
not in culottes, but in long flowing skirts,
gliding erect through early morning mists.

Back at home in the Rue de Boulogne,
his care for fact, for Dreyfus, justified,
his valet laid a fire to warm his bed:
windows shut tight, he placed within the grate
a type of smokeless, coal briquette.

In sleep he breathed carbon monoxide,
murdered perhaps. We'll never know;
maybe an accident, although
years later a man decided to repent,
and said he'd blocked the chimney vent.

After pompous funeral rites they found
his fortune much reduced, and so his wife
sold objects which composed his daily life,
auctioned his rich paraphernalia,
selling off stained glass, paintings, furniture,

and nine Cézannes. For twenty years she watched
her Zola, like the paintings, grow in worth,
landscapes rippling, vibrant, echoes of a truth,
while she spent money helping Jeanne to rear
the children she herself could never bear.

A Chekhov Tale

Moscow captured, held still
beneath a weight of snow.

Under the crystal stars
students, crunching ice, go

across the moonlit streets
to ancient brothels, where

flunkeys in black frock-coats,
behind red portières,

unshaven, sleepy-eyed,
take roubles for entry.

A laundry smell surrounds
girls with giggles, each knee

winking slyly at men
who pay up cash for beer.

Thick make-up, collars smeared
scarlet, the girls appear

like dolls displayed in shops.
The students, shy, don't dare

to pay the money due
and mount the final stair.

Under the watching moon,
the lamp God left behind,

they fantasise they'll make
each prostitute a friend,

save them from brothel slush
in summer palaces.

Above, a last star fades.
Snow holds them in its arms.

Walter Benjamin, 1940

Yours should have been a Hollywood escape;
ingredients were all to hand:
a portly, left-wing Mayor, Azema,

who offered you a scribbled map
through vineyards to the promised land,
And Lisa Fittko, heroine, your guide,

ardent Jewess before whose eyes
wild hills bow down and rivers part.
And you, the awkward scholar role,

in danger from your ailing heart.
Instead, your papers incomplete,
the squalor of your suicide;

the manuscript you lugged across
high stony paths, past border guards,
has disappeared, our total loss.

On this autumn day in the Pyrenees
old mountain ways to freedom don't exist:
history without progress, just a list.

I see you stumbling downhill to Port Bou,
in extremity conventionally polite,
like old-world Berlin Jews
who doffed their hats to every passer-by.

Autun in the Middle Ages

On Sundays peasants witnessed Hell:
tympanum of Gislebertus;
beneath robed Christ in Majesty
the resurrection of the damned:

a lustful lady's breasts devoured
by serpents, Avarice dragged down
into the pit, his fortune tied
around his neck, huge devil's claws

seizing a sinner by the throat.
So, as the congregation walked
through fields to home, they bore with them
stark images of twisted souls.

And yet, from what we read, they still
fornicated, just like us,
slandered neighbours, just like us,
unfazed by the real fear of Hell.

Plum-blossom fell on children's graves,
so many forced to die so young.
The peasants knew the daily round,
that children dead are children lost,

and all the talk of punishment
or God's rewards not relevant
when standing by an open grave.

Quinta del Sordo

Goya bought a mansion,
fountain and small vineyard
for a handsome gentlewoman
whose sharp-tongued words
he never heard.

In the silence of home
he lived inside his dreams,
daily routines
beside huge murals in oil,
fearsome scenes.

Judith's raised knife,
Saturn's bloody maw;
under poisonous clouds
darkness closes
on frightened crowds.

Now in the Prado
I view his private hell,
agape at mobs, witch, imbecile,
murderous Spanish wars:
corpses on a barren hill.

Outside in Parque del Retiro
in fierce sunlight
his images recede.
I watch children, carefree
as if there's no tomorrow.

Sometimes it's better to be deaf;
sometimes it hurts so much to see.

The Grand Hotel, Taiwan

Without my wife, my newspaper,
I'm glum. Holed up in a hideaway
Chiang Kai-shek built above Taipei

I'm plagued at dawn by dragons,
writhing around crimson pillars,
entwined in lattice-work designs.

Their golden, five-pronged talons
threaten my patchy slumbers
in this mock hotel on epic lines,

suited to dreams of warriors, not to me,
guest lecturer far from home,
missing his morning cup of tea.

From my balcony I survey Taipei.
Ancient dragons of China flew
to fetch sweet rain to swell the crops,

gobbled no virgins, only slew
wicked merchants, while today
silver Boeing after Boeing drops

through city smog, over sweatshops,
into the crowded coils of motorways.
Confucius taught respect for words,

meaning to be restored to clichés:
goods should be truly good,
husbands act as husbands,

rulers as sages. I need clean air,
so walk up steps into a scraggy wood,
a busy peasant thoroughfare,

past advertisements, coca-cola stands,
badminton courts, a stone Buddha, to where
in a bower of cedars an old man

keeps a stall for drawings and calligraphy.
He explains his craft in English
with simple truth and courtesy.

I admire each careful brush stroke,
his trust in nature and in words,
an artist who respects his art:

his blue-scaled dragons sweep the sky
as lively as a wheeling flock of birds.